BOOK
ONE

Palmer-Hughes

SPINET ORGAN COURSE

by Bill Palmer and Bill Hughes

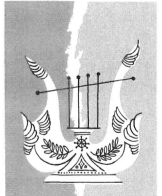

EDUCATIONAL MUSIC PUBLISHERS *Alfred Music* CO., INC.,

FOREWORD

IF YOU ARE A BEGINNER, whether young or old, and if you would like to learn to play the Spinet Organ correctly, *BY NOTE*, this book is for you!

Notes seem a bit frightening to most people who have had no experience with them, but actually *IT IS EASIER TO LEARN TO PLAY BY NOTE THAN ANY OTHER WAY*. If this were not true, the present system of musical notation would not have survived over the centuries.

The *PALMER-HUGHES SPINET ORGAN COURSE* introduces the principles of note reading in the most simple, careful and logical manner possible.

Finger numbers are emphasized at the beginning, but only so that you can learn good fingering habits, coordinate quickly and correctly, and produce musical results immediately. But this is *NOT A READ-BY-NUMBER METHOD!* As soon as the basic coordination problems are mastered, you will learn to *READ ENTIRELY BY NOTE*, without using the "crutch" of finger numbers.

By the time you have finished this book you will be able to instantly recognize every note and every chord used in this book. You will be able to coordinate the two hands with the pedal in playing many familiar selections *BY NOTE*.

The Publishers

STUDY THIS BOOK CAREFULLY, MASTERING EACH EASY STEP AS YOU GO, AND YOU WILL BE ON YOUR WAY TO THE MOST COMPLETE ENJOYMENT OF YOUR SPINET ORGAN.

Note to TEACHERS

CHORDS USED IN THIS BOOK ARE IN VARIOUS INVERSIONS, SO THAT THEY MAKE GOOD PROGRESSIONS, AND SO THAT THE LEFT HAND DOES NOT HAVE TO MOVE FROM ONE BASIC POSITION.
THREE NOTE SEVENTH CHORDS (WITH THE FIFTH OMITTED) ARE USED FOR THE SAKE OF SIMPLICITY, AND BECAUSE THEY MAKE BETTER PROGRESSIONS TO THE MAJOR TRIADS.

TABLE OF CONTENTS

REGISTRATION •

Registration for the selections in this book is left to the discretion of the teacher or the student. The authors of this book recommend that the registration be kept BASIC and SIMPLE.

THE FOLLOWING REGISTRATION WILL PROVE EFFECTIVE FOR ALL THE SELECTIONS IN THIS BOOK:

NORMAL VIBRATO

REVERBERATION (if available)

Any SOLO tone; TRUMPET, CLARINET or FULL ORGAN
(for the UPPER MANUAL)

Any ENSEMBLE tone, a bit softer than the above solo tone
(for the LOWER MANUAL)

The student will find added enjoyment in experimenting with various tonal combinations. The same selection may be played several times, with a different registration each time. The Owner's Manual or Guide will be helpful in providing suggestions for effective registration.

Sacred selections, such as the "ODE TO JOY" are considered by some people to be more effective with *NO VIBRATO*. Such things are best left to the personal taste of the organist.

The authors believe that students who experiment with registration learn more about the instrument they are playing than those who simply go by the suggested registration at the top of most copies of sheet music. Such registration usually represents the personal taste of the editor or arranger, and does not have to be observed for a correct rendition of the music. The exception, of course, is in playing music composed especially for organ, when the composer himself has selected the registration. Such compositions for Spinet Organ are so rare that they do not even need to be considered here.

☞ IMPORTANT!

THE EXPRESSION PEDAL (SWELL PEDAL)

To the right of the pedal keyboard is the *EXPRESSION PEDAL*, which is operated with the RIGHT FOOT. This pedal must be partially depressed for the sound of the organ to be audible.

It is not necessary to vary the touch on the keyboards to increase or decrease the volume of sound. This is done with the *EXPRESSION PEDAL*. Press FORWARD with the front part of the foot to INCREASE the volume of sound. Press BACK with the heel of the foot to DECREASE the volume. *EXPRESSION* in this book is left to the discretion of the teacher or student.

MORE DETAILED USE OF THE EXPRESSION PEDAL WILL BE TAKEN UP IN LATER PALMER-HUGHES ORGAN BOOKS.

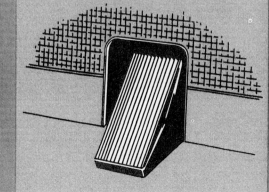

LOCATING THE C 's

Notice that each MANUAL or KEYBOARD has the same pattern of BLACK KEYS repeated over and over:

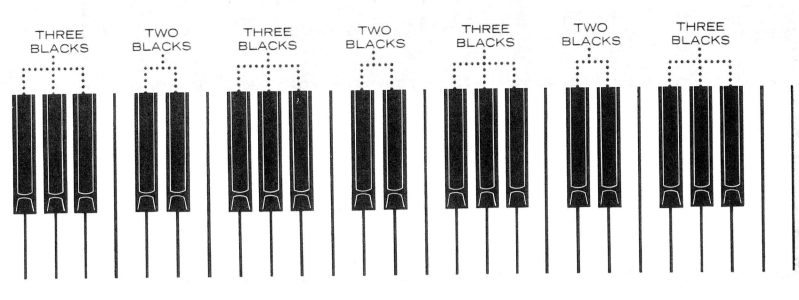

THREE BLACKS   TWO BLACKS   THREE BLACKS   TWO BLACKS   THREE BLACKS   TWO BLACKS   THREE BLACKS

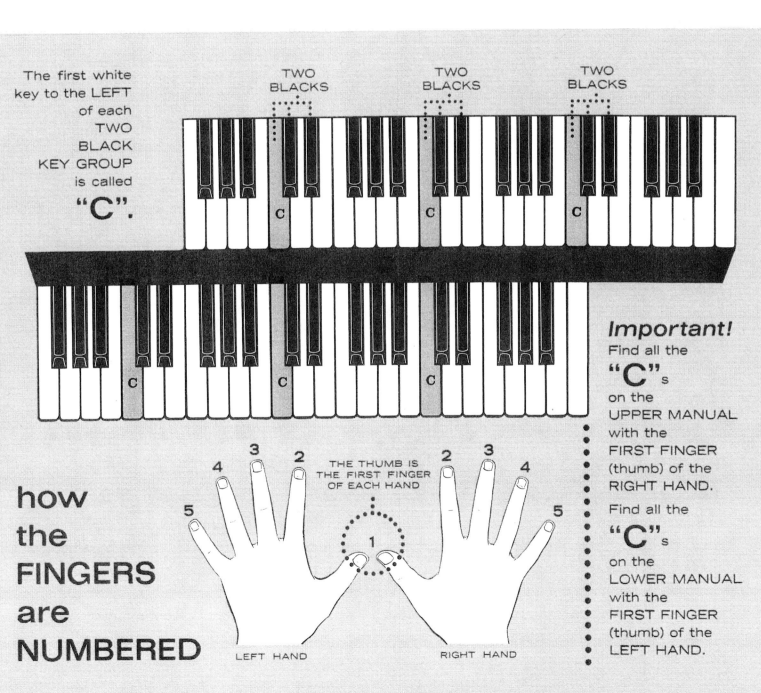

The first white key to the LEFT of each TWO BLACK KEY GROUP is called "C".

TWO BLACKS   TWO BLACKS   TWO BLACKS

how the FINGERS are NUMBERED

THE THUMB IS THE FIRST FINGER OF EACH HAND

LEFT HAND   RIGHT HAND

Important!
Find all the "C"s on the UPPER MANUAL with the FIRST FINGER (thumb) of the RIGHT HAND.

Find all the "C"s on the LOWER MANUAL with the FIRST FINGER (thumb) of the LEFT HAND.

RIGHT HAND POSITION

Place the
RIGHT HAND
on the
UPPER MANUAL
so the
THUMB
is on the
FIRST C.

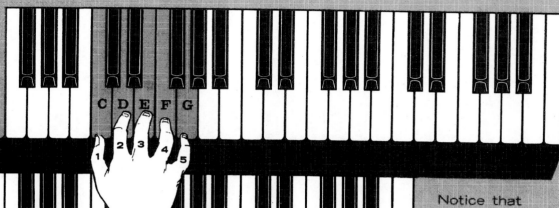

Notice that
the NAMES
of the
five notes
are in
ALPHABETICAL
ORDER:
C D E F G

The FIRST FINGER (thumb) is on C.
The SECOND FINGER is on D.
The THIRD FINGER is on E.
The FOURTH FINGER is on F.
The FIFTH FINGER is on G.

MUSIC FOR THE
UPPER MANUAL IS
WRITTEN ON A STAFF OF FIVE LINES

TREBLE CLEF
SIGN MEANS
PLAY ON
UPPER MANUAL

This diagram shows
how the names of
the NOTES match the
names of the KEYS:

RIGHT HAND "WARM-UP"

With the hand in the same position play the following "WARM-UP". *USE THE FINGER NUMBERS* to tell you which keys to press. Repeat until you can play SMOOTHLY:

Merrily We Roll Along

As you play this familiar melody you may use the *NUMBERS*, which tell you which finger to play. You may also begin to notice the *NOTES* below the numbers.

LEFT HAND POSITION

Place the
LEFT HAND
on the
LOWER MANUAL
so the
SECOND FINGER
is on the
SECOND C.

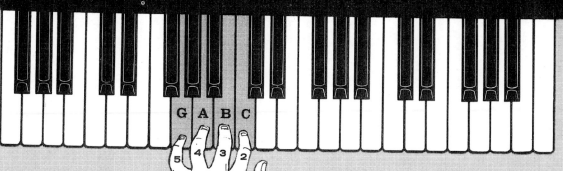

Notice that the
NAMES of the
four notes are
G A B C

The SECOND FINGER is on C.
The THIRD FINGER is on B.
The FOURTH FINGER is on A.
The FIFTH FINGER is on G.

MUSIC FOR THE LOWER MANUAL IS WRITTEN ON A STAFF OF FIVE LINES

BASS CLEF
SIGN MEANS
PLAY ON
LOWER MANUAL

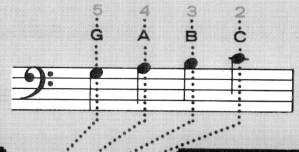

This diagram shows how the
names of the NOTES match
the names of the KEYS of
the LOWER MANUAL:

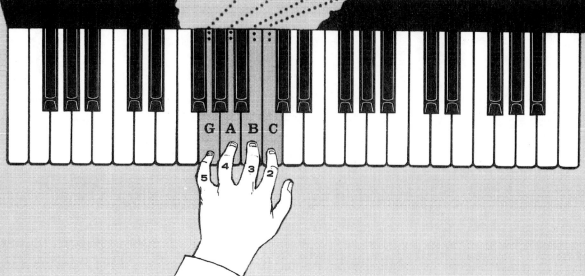

LEFT HAND "WARM-UP"

With the hand in the same position play the following "WARM-UP". *USE THE FINGER NUMBERS* to tell you which keys to press. Repeat until you can play SMOOTHLY:

The LEFT HAND usually plays CHORDS (two or more notes at the same time) to accompany the right hand melody. *WE WILL BEGIN WITH TWO-NOTE CHORDS.*

1. PLAY THE 5th and 2nd FINGERS TOGETHER (on G and C).
2. PLAY THE 5th and 3rd FINGERS TOGETHER (on G and B).

ACCOMPANIMENT "WARM-UP"

In this ACCOMPANIMENT you may use the NUMBERS to tell you which fingers to play. You may also notice the notes beside the numbers, if you wish. These notes will be studied more thoroughly later.

Now play the following, *HOLDING THE 5th FINGER DOWN* for the entire exercise:

The curved lines (TIES) indicate that the 5th finger is HELD DOWN (not struck again).

9

PLAYING  and  TOGETHER

UPPER MANUAL

LOWER MANUAL

UPPER MANUAL ▶

◀ **LOWER MANUAL**

PLAY THE FIRST RIGHT HAND NOTE (E) EXACTLY WITH THE LEFT HAND NOTES (G AND C).

Continue to hold the LEFT HAND NOTES DOWN while you play all the RIGHT HAND NOTES.

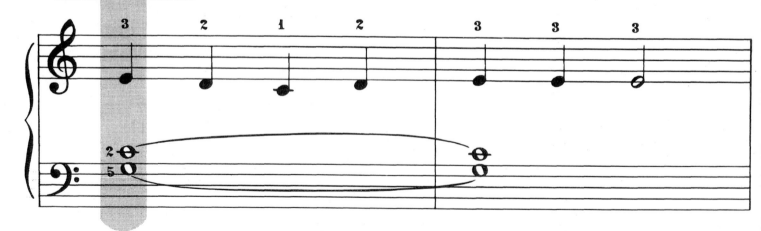

These curved lines (TIES) indicate that the second chord is HELD DOWN (not struck again).

TIES

Merrily We Roll Along (HANDS TOGETHER)

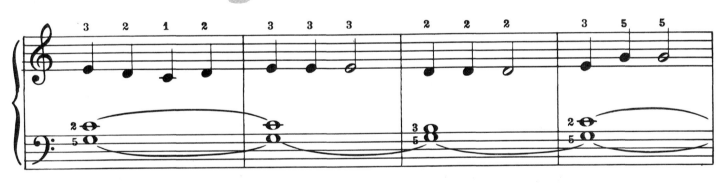

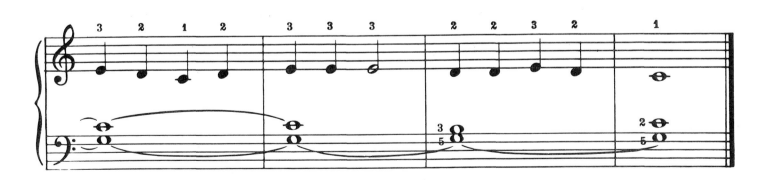

11

INTRODUCING D and E FOR THE LEFT HAND

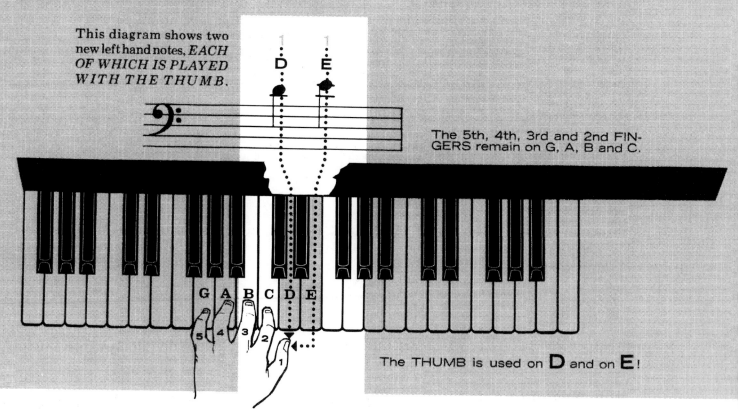

This diagram shows two new left hand notes, *EACH OF WHICH IS PLAYED WITH THE THUMB.*

The 5th, 4th, 3rd and 2nd FINGERS remain on G, A, B and C.

The THUMB is used on D and on E!

THE TWO MOST IMPORTANT CHORDS...

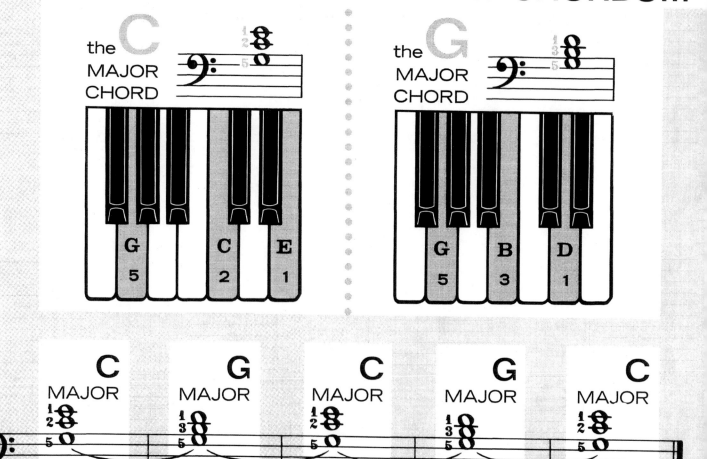

the C MAJOR CHORD

the G MAJOR CHORD

KEEP THE LITTLE FINGER DOWN FOR THE ENTIRE EXERCISE!

CHORD ABBREVIATIONS:

C indicates the C MAJOR CHORD.

G indicates the G MAJOR CHORD.

These symbols will appear *ABOVE THE TREBLE STAFF* of each selection, as is customary in most organ music. It is desirable to know the left hand chords well enough to play them by merely using these symbols. It is also *NECESSARY* to be able to read the left hand notes. For the present, you may use the FINGER NUMBERS NEXT TO THE LEFT HAND NOTES.

Merrily We Roll Along ..(WITH THREE-NOTE CHORDS!)

INTRODUCING THE PEDALS

The PEDAL NOTES are arranged in the same order as the notes of the manuals. There is a *TWO BLACK KEY GROUP* and a *THREE BLACK KEY GROUP*. The note to the LEFT of the *TWO BLACK KEY GROUP* is C. (This is the FIRST PEDAL.) The FIFTH LONG PEDAL is G. You will see that the pedals are like a short third keyboard.

PEDAL REGISTRATION

PEDAL VOLUME or PEDAL REGISTRATION should be selected to balance with the notes played on the manuals.

Avoid having the pedals too soft, particularly at the beginning of the study of the pedals. Be sure that the volume is loud enough so that the pitch of each pedal note is clearly audible.

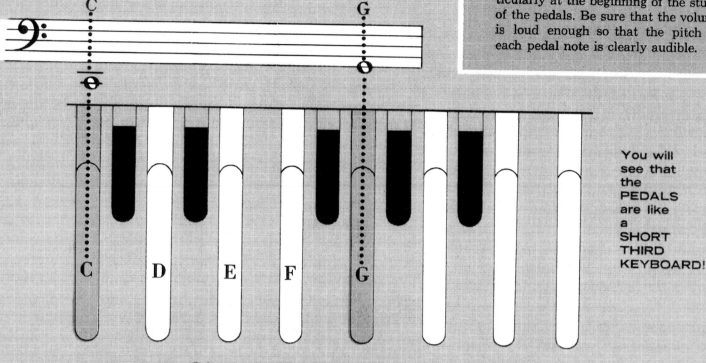

You will see that the PEDALS are like a SHORT THIRD KEYBOARD!

NOTICE!   C is on the SECOND short line (leger line) below the bass staff.
G is on the FIRST (lowest) line of the bass staff.

YOU SHOULD LEARN

TO READ THE **C** AND **G** PEDAL NOTES **NOW** BY RECOGNITION!

PLAY THE PEDAL NOTES **C** AND **G** WITH THE TOE OF THE LEFT FOOT.

To facilitate the location of the G pedal, without looking at the feet, you should be seated on the organ bench in such a position that your left foot is directly in front of the G pedal!

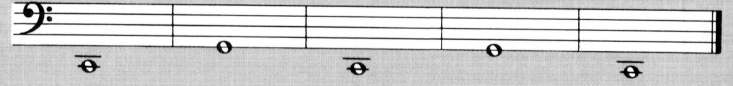

NOW PLAY THE LEFT HAND AND THE PEDAL TOGETHER

NOTICE!   The C PEDAL is used when the LEFT HAND plays the C MAJOR CHORD.
The G PEDAL is used when the LEFT HAND plays the G MAJOR CHORD.

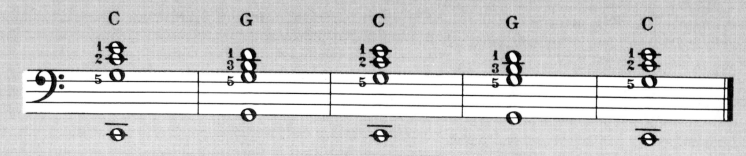

Some organ music is written on TWO STAFFS, with the upper manual on the upper staff, and the *lower manual and pedals* on the lower staff. More advanced organ music is sometimes written on THREE STAFFS, with a separate staff provided for the lower manual, and a separate one for the pedals.

For the sake of simplification, we will begin with TWO STAFFS. Later in the course three staffs will be used.

Merrily We Roll Along... (FOR TWO MANUALS AND PEDAL)

Hold each pedal note until the chord changes, as indicated by the ties!

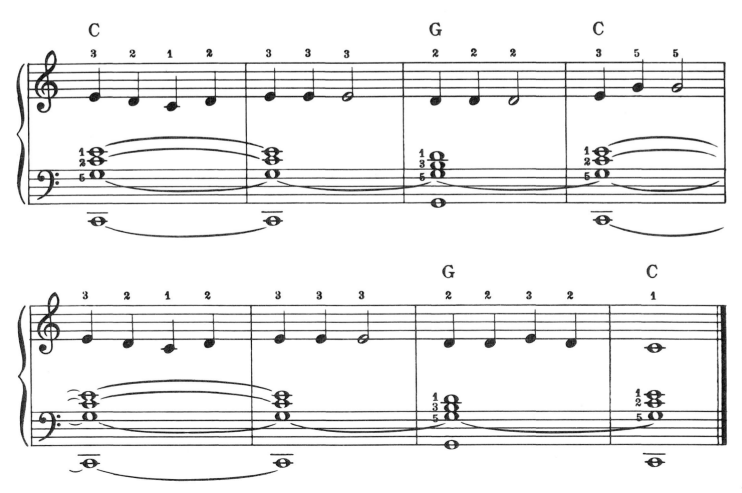

MORE ABOUT MUSIC READING

At this point you should begin to read the music of the treble staff WITHOUT USING FINGER NUMBERS!

You will remember that music is written on a STAFF of FIVE LINES.

The TREBLE CLEF SIGN at the beginning of the staff tells you that the notes on that staff are to be played on the UPPER MANUAL.

In the example below, notice that the BAR LINES divide the music into MEASURES. A DOUBLE BAR is used at the END of a piece.

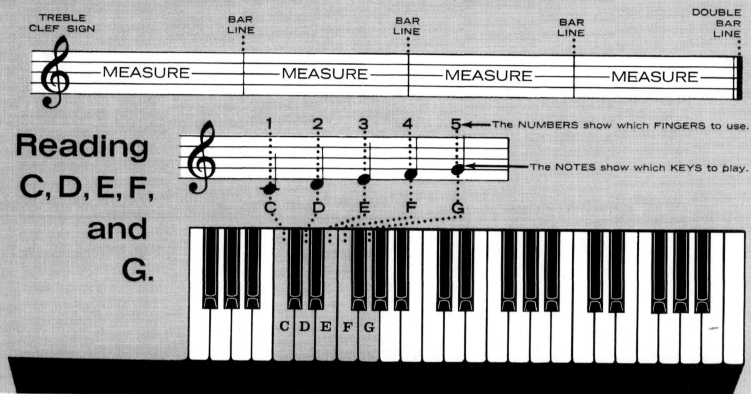

Reading C, D, E, F, and G.

The following three lines of music work like... MAGIC to give you a good start in note reading.

1. NAME EACH NOTE
2. PLAY EACH NOTE

16

Largo
from "THE NEW WORLD"
DVORAK

FINGER NUMBERS
ARE
PURPOSELY OMITTED!

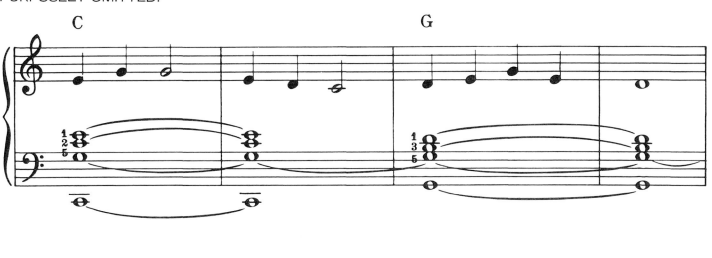

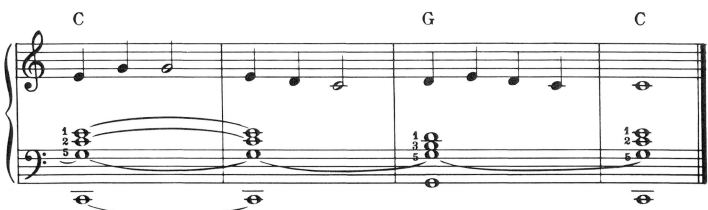

RHYTHM (HOW TO COUNT TIME)

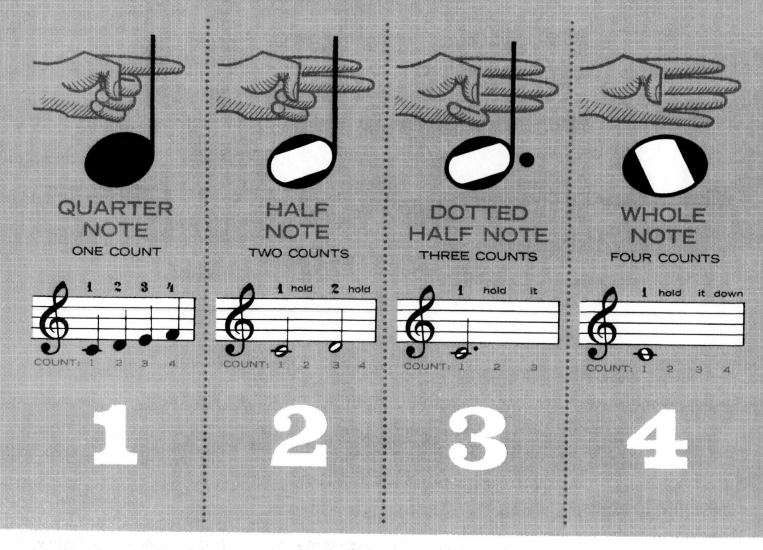

QUARTER NOTE	HALF NOTE	DOTTED HALF NOTE	WHOLE NOTE
ONE COUNT	TWO COUNTS	THREE COUNTS	FOUR COUNTS

1 2 3 4

THE TIME SIGNATURE

Each piece of music should have numbers at the beginning, called TIME SIGNATURES which tell us how to count time.

COUNT FOUR TO EACH MEASURE

A QUARTER NOTE GETS ONE COUNT

LIGHTLY ROW...

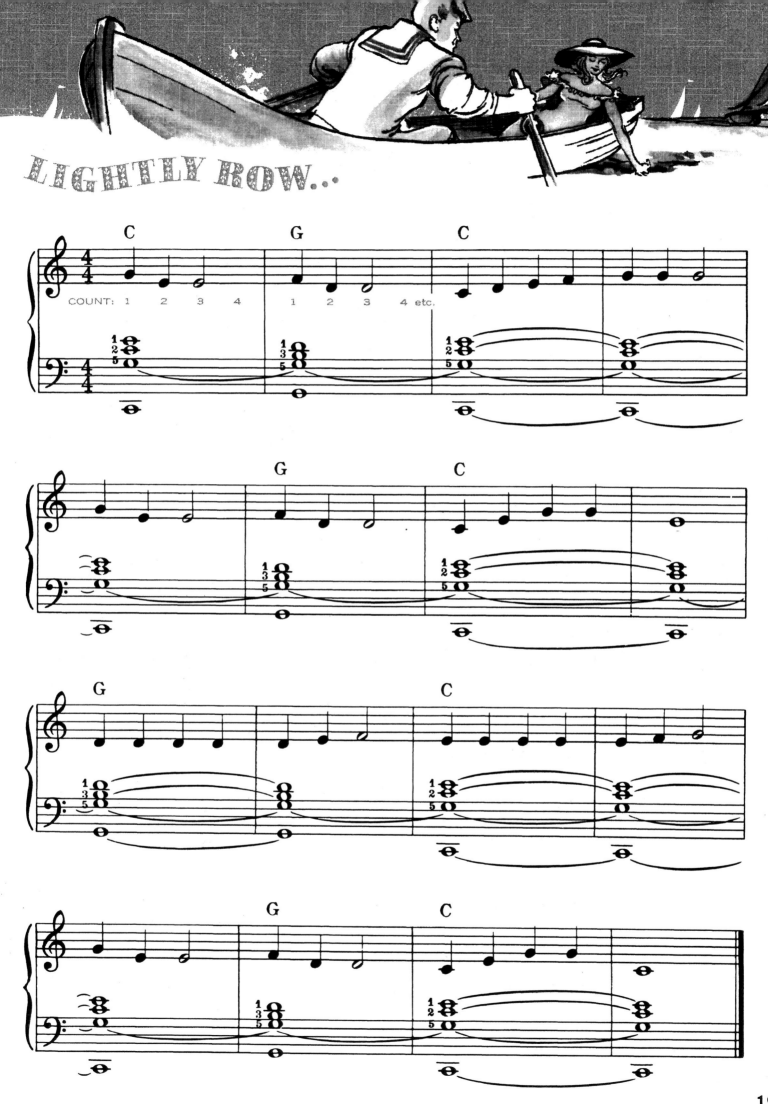

INTRODUCING F FOR THE LEFT HAND

This diagram introduces one new left hand note, F, which is played with the THUMB.

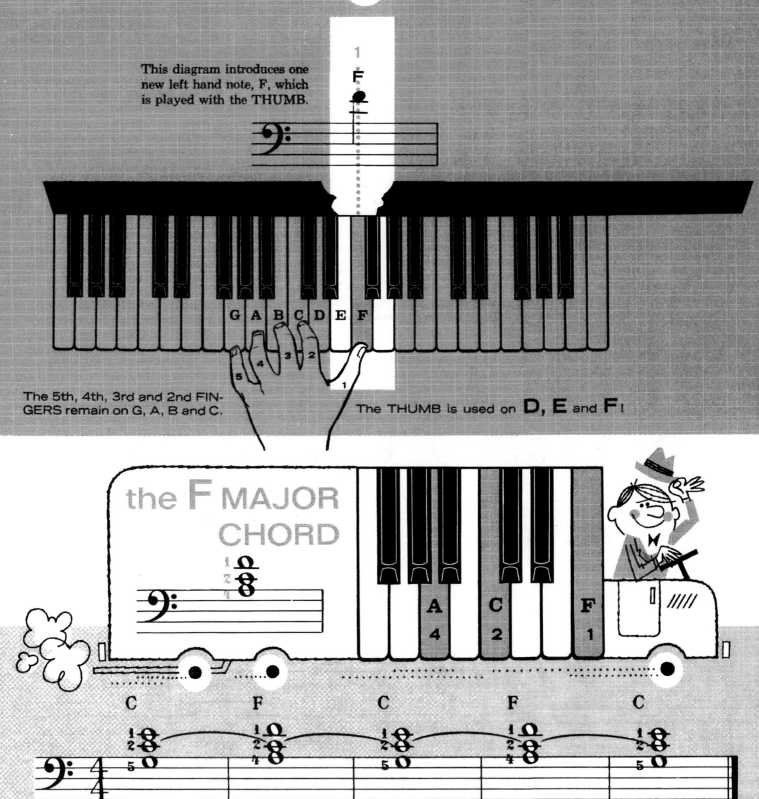

The 5th, 4th, 3rd and 2nd FINGERS remain on G, A, B and C.

The THUMB is used on D, E and F!

the F MAJOR CHORD

NOTE: *HOLD THE C DOWN (with the 2nd finger) WHEN CHANGING FROM C MAJOR TO F MAJOR, OR VICE-VERSA.*

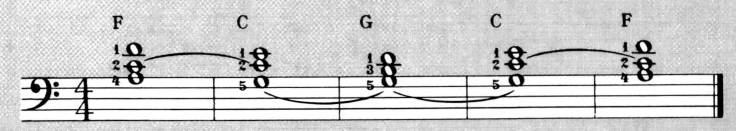

INTRODUCING THE ⓕ PEDAL

The FOURTH LONG PEDAL is F. The F PEDAL is indicated on the music by a note on the SPACE JUST BELOW the bass staff.

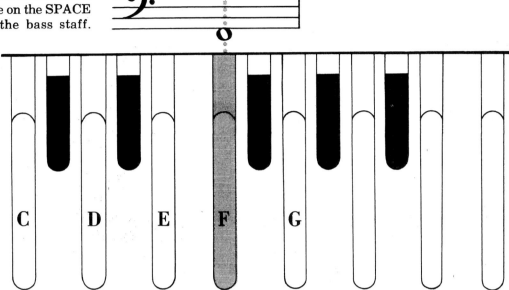

ALWAYS LOOK AT YOUR MUSIC!

Practice playing the C, F and G pedals without looking at the feet. Use the right side of the toe to feel the left side of the black-key pedal near the pedal you wish to play. This will guide you in finding the correct pedal while you keep your eyes ON THE MUSIC.

COUNT: 1 2 3 4   1 2 3 4   etc.

The F PEDAL
is used when the LEFT HAND plays the F MAJOR CHORD!

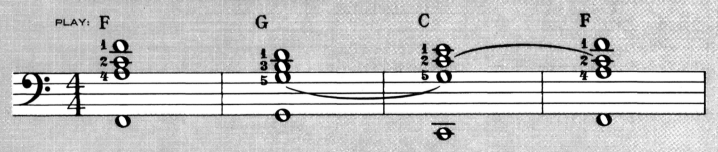

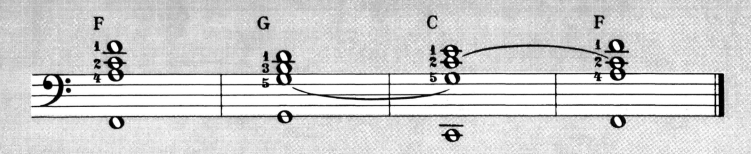

AURA LEE

(LOVE ME TRULY)

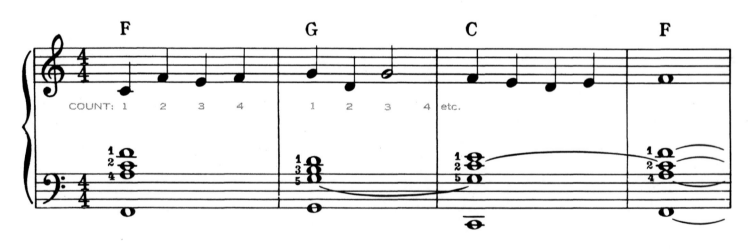

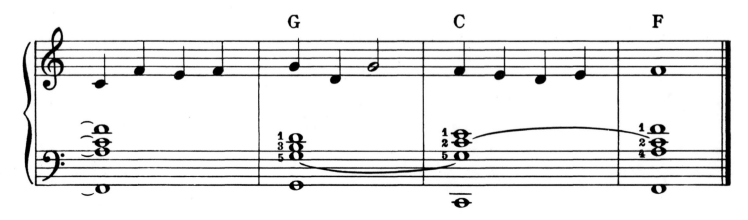

A NEW TIME SIGNATURE

A GREAT DEAL OF POPULAR MUSIC, AS WELL AS CLASSICAL MUSIC, IS WRITTEN IN $\frac{3}{4}$ TIME.

COUNT THREE TO EACH MEASURE

A QUARTER NOTE GETS ONE COUNT

IN ANY TIME SIGNATURE: The TOP NUMBER tells you the NUMBER OF COUNTS IN A MEASURE.
The BOTTOM NUMBER tells you the KIND OF NOTE that gets ONE COUNT.

Preparation for "BEAUTIFUL BROWN EYES"

Play this right hand melody, counting slowly, evenly, and LOUDLY! *REMEMBER!* The second note of TIED NOTES is HELD DOWN (not struck again)!

Beautiful Brown Eyes

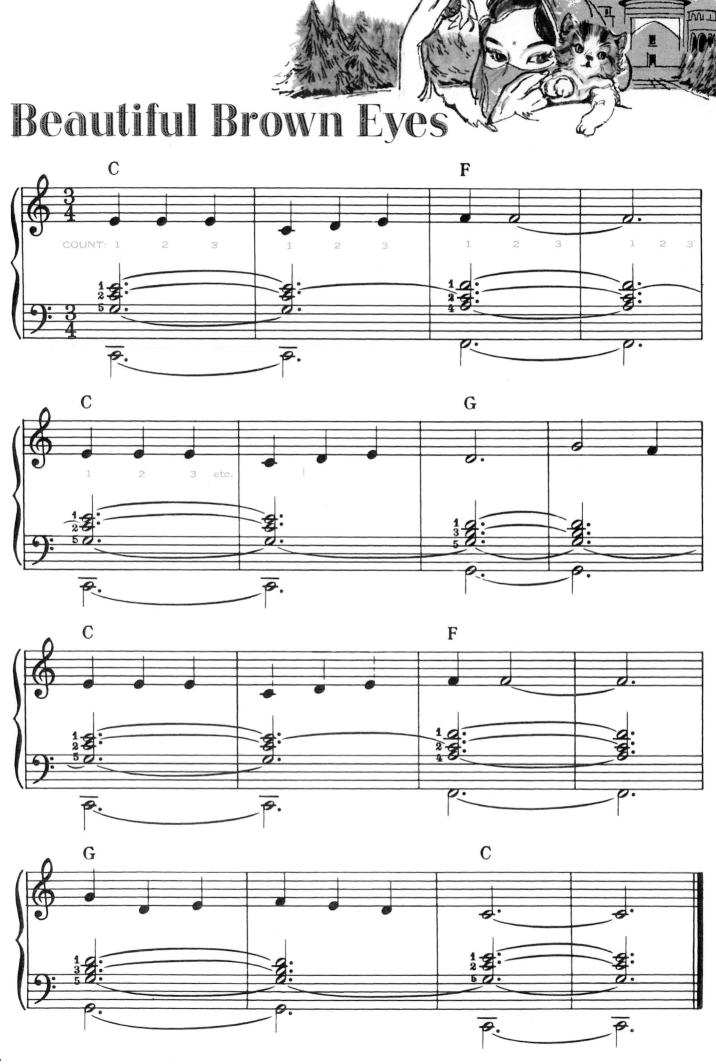

READING CHORDS BY RECOGNITION

So far, you have played these THREE LEFT HAND CHORDS:

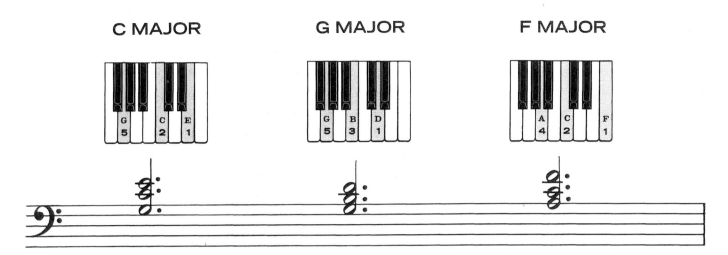

C MAJOR   G MAJOR   F MAJOR

It is very important that you know these three chords BY NAME, so that you are able to play them referring only to the SYMBOLS (chord names) that are printed just above the treble staff. *It is also very important* that you know these three chords BY RECOGNITION. That is, you *must* be able to recognize each chord by its appearance on the staff.

PLAY THESE LINES OF MUSIC, NAMING EACH CHORD ALOUD AS YOU PLAY: (Fingering numbers are purposely omitted).

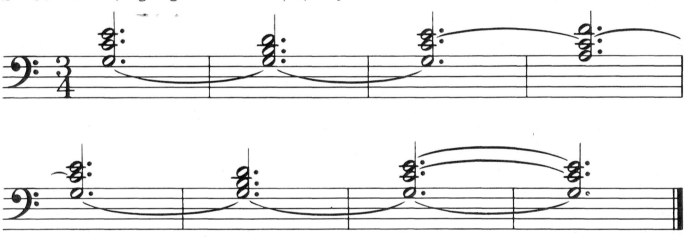

NOW ADD THE PEDALS, ALSO BY RECOGNITION:

25

Drink To Me Only With Thine Eyes

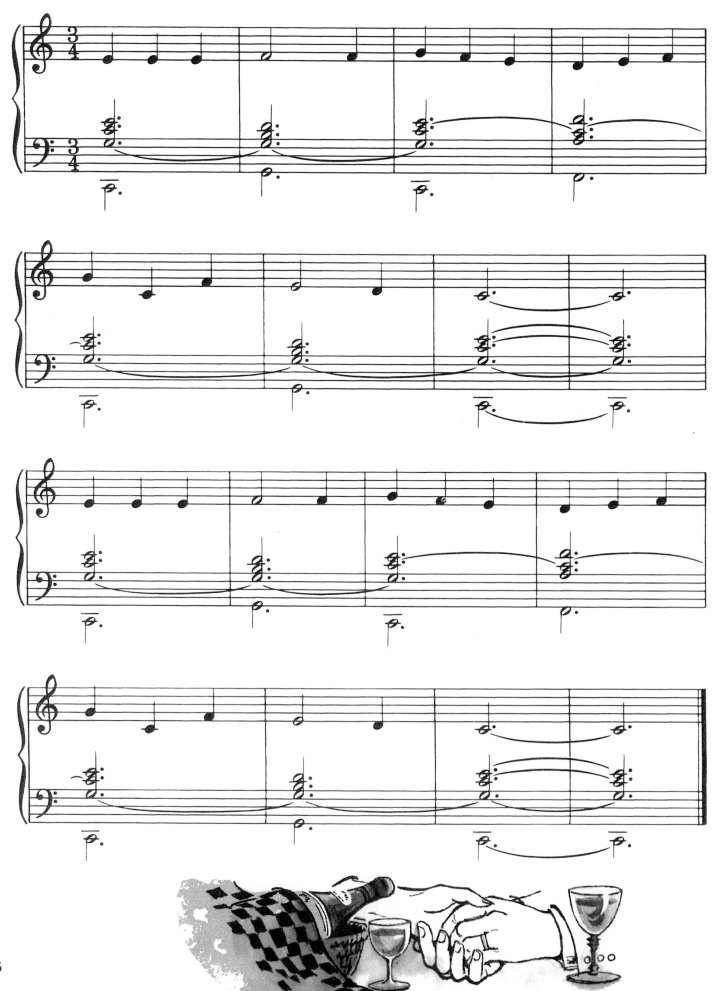

*THE G SEVENTH CHORD

From G to F is a span of SEVEN NOTES. For this reason, this chord is called a G SEVENTH CHORD (abbreviated G7).

THE G PEDAL IS USED WITH THE G7 CHORD.

Ode to Joy

(THEME FROM THE NINTH SYMPHONY)

BEETHOVEN

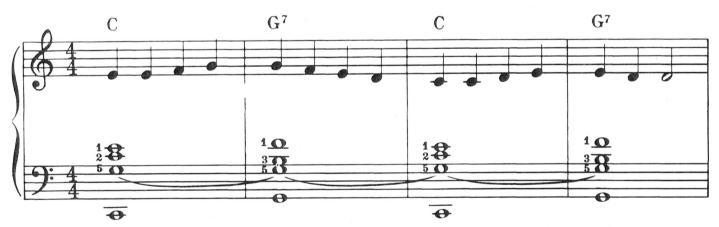

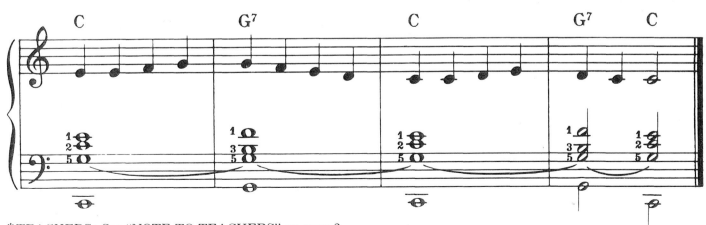

*TEACHERS: See "NOTE TO TEACHERS" on page 2.

27

RECOGNIZING THE G⁷ CHORD

Note carefully the difference between the G MAJOR and the G SEVENTH CHORDS:

• ONE WHITE KEY •

BETWEEN 3 AND 1

• THREE WHITE KEYS •

BETWEEN 3 AND 1

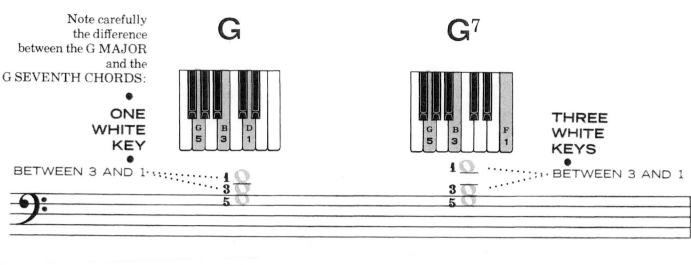

• • • • • • •

CHORD REVIEW

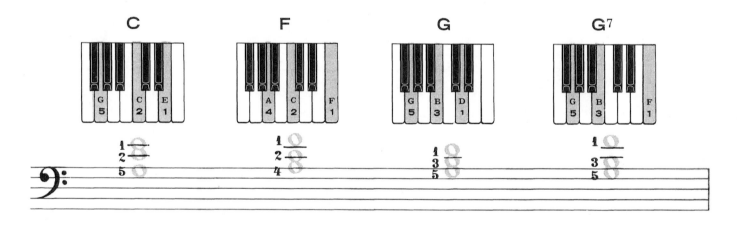

THIS EXERCISE IS A REVIEW OF ALL THE CHORDS STUDIED IN THIS BOOK:

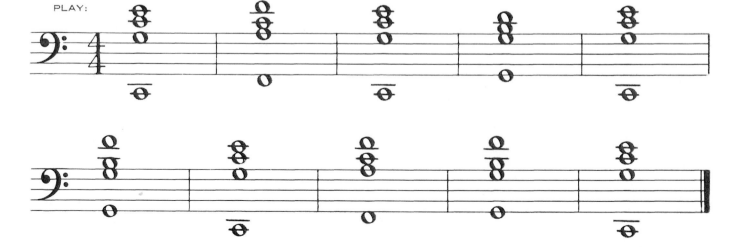

QUARTER REST
(SILENCE FOR ONE COUNT)

INCOMPLETE MEASURE:

Note that the first measure is incomplete. Start on the third count. The 1st and 2nd counts are found in the last measure.

HI-LEE, HI-LO

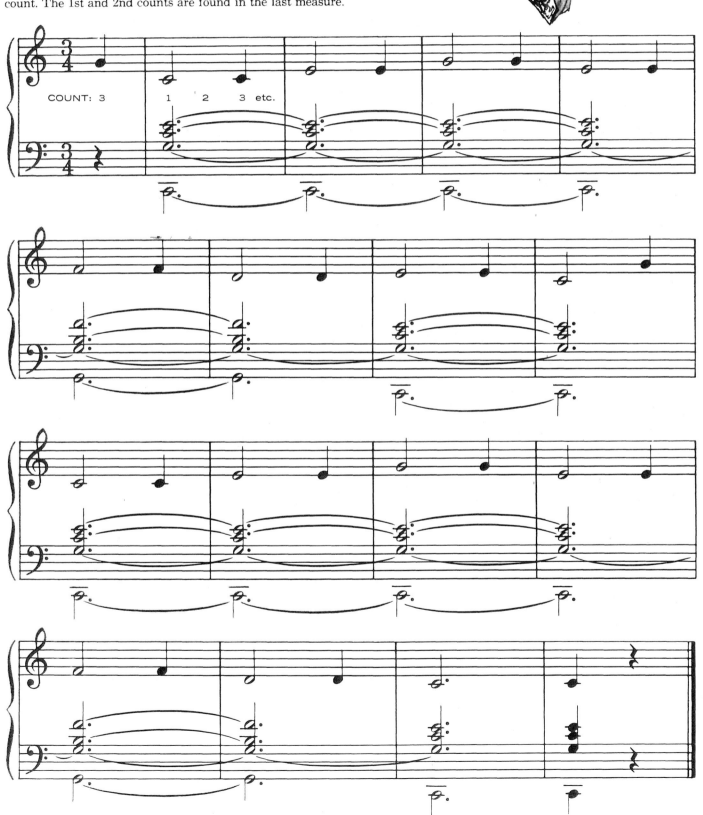

COUNT: 3   1   2   3 etc.

POP!
Goes the Weasel

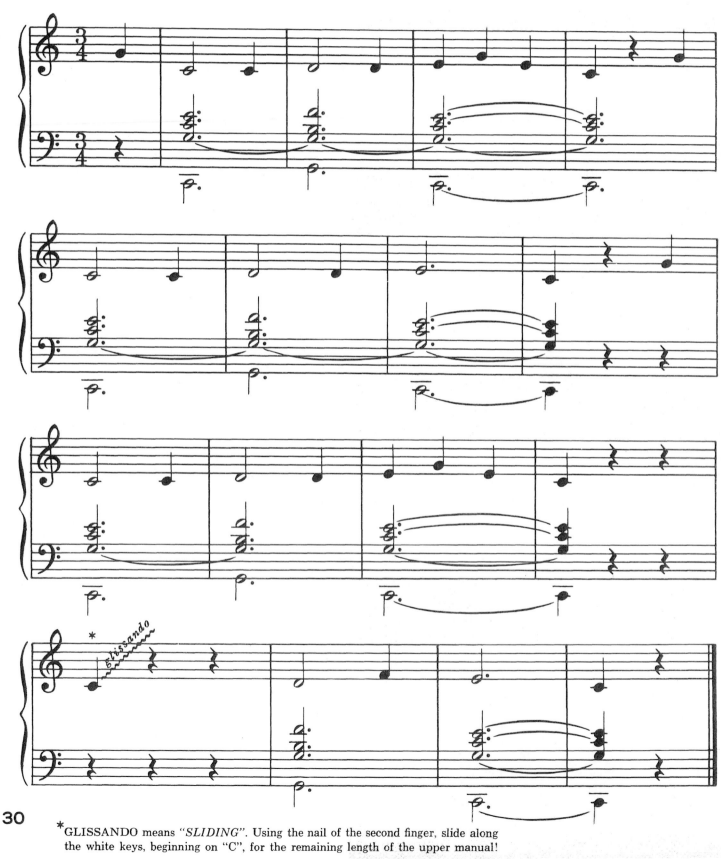

*GLISSANDO means "SLIDING". Using the nail of the second finger, slide along
the white keys, beginning on "C", for the remaining length of the upper manual!

Red River Valley

(FIVE FINGER VERSION)

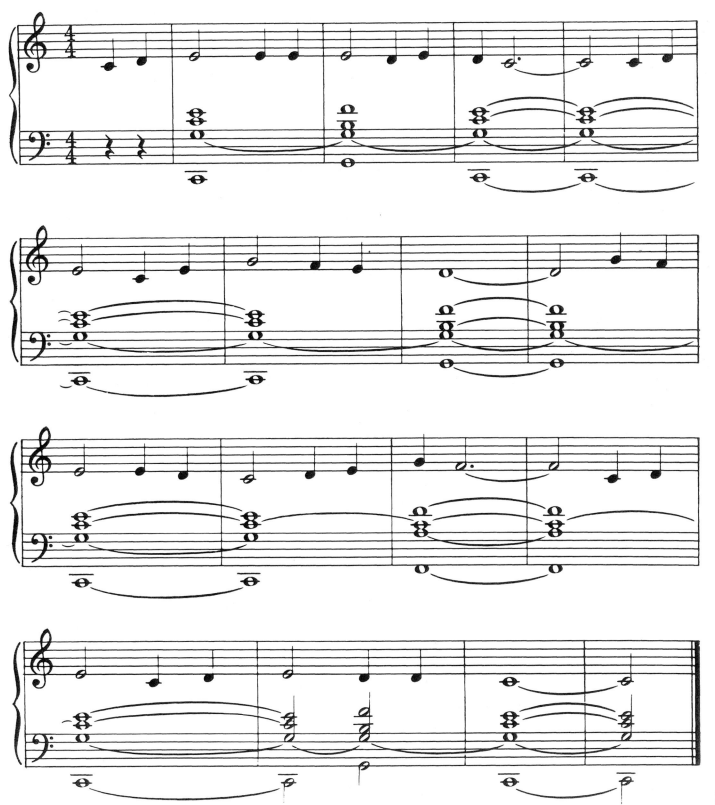

QUIZ

 1. THIS IS A_____CLEF SIGN. 𝄢 THIS IS A_____CLEF SIGN.

2. THE_____CLEF SIGN IS USED FOR THE LOWER MANUAL AND PEDALS.

3. THE_____CLEF SIGN IS USED FOR THE UPPER MANUAL.

4. WRITE THE NAMES OF THE FOLLOWING NOTES:

_____ _____ _____ _____ _____

5. WRITE THE NAMES OF THE FOLLOWING CHORDS:

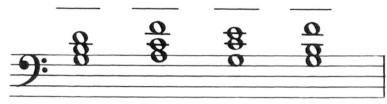

6. **3/4** THIS TIME SIGNATURE MEANS COUNT_____TO EACH MEASURE.

7. **4/4** THIS TIME SIGNATURE MEANS COUNT_____TO EACH MEASURE.

8. WHEN TWO NOTES ON THE SAME LINE OR SPACE ARE CONNECTED BY A CURVED LINE ‿ THEY ARE CALLED _____ NOTES.

9. WRITE THE NUMBER OF COUNTS EACH NOTE RECEIVES:

_____ _____ _____ _____

10. WRITE THE NAMES OF THE FOLLOWING PEDAL NOTES:

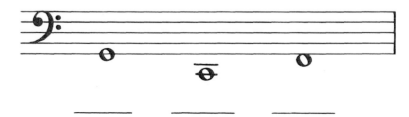

_____ _____ _____ _____

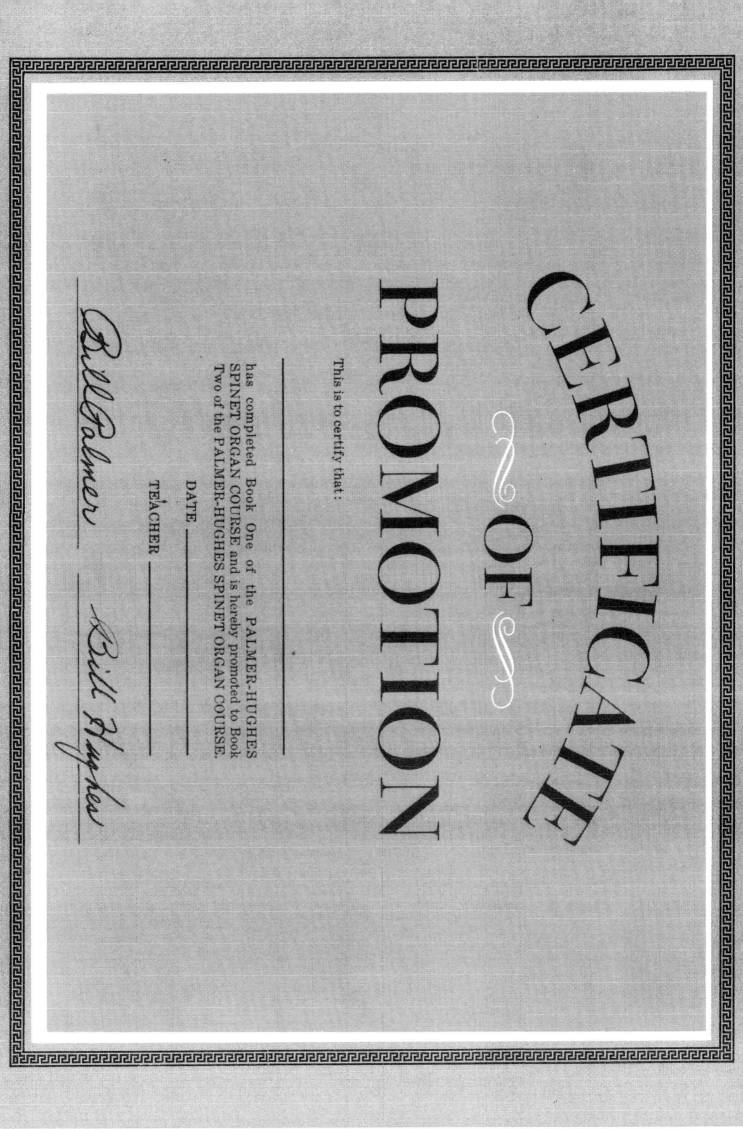

CERTIFICATE
OF
PROMOTION

This is to certify that:

_____

has completed Book One of the PALMER-HUGHES
SPINET ORGAN COURSE and is hereby promoted to Book
Two of the PALMER-HUGHES SPINET ORGAN COURSE.

DATE _____

TEACHER _____

Bill Palmer

Bill Hughes

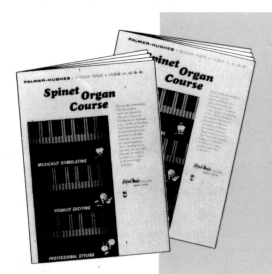

Palmer-Hughes
Spinet Organ Courses

SPINET ORGAN COURSE (all organs)	HAMMOND ORGAN COURSE
BOOK 1	BOOK 1
BOOK 2	BOOK 2
BOOK 3	BOOK 3
BOOK 4	BOOK 4
BOOK 5	BOOK 5
BOOK 6	BOOK 6

AT LAST! A Spinet Organ Course that teaches the student to play correctly, *by note*. The student also learns to play chords in the inversions that sound best and which progress smoothly from one to another without awkward skips!

In the later books, the student learns to play and recognize chords in all positions, and to read music over the entire range of both manuals and the pedal keyboard.

This course was designed to provide proper but pleasureable instruction for students of all ages. One edition is for all spinet organs while the other is specifically for Hammond Spinet Organs.

EASIEST HYMN BOOK

You can play every hymn in this book by using only 8 notes on the upper manual, 4 chords on the lower manual and 3 pedals for half the book, 5 altogether.

HOOTENANNY ORGAN BOOK

Here is a complete Hootenanny program in one book! Not just a collection of random folk songs, but an authentic variety put in Hootenanny sequence. Extra cut-out lyrics.

JAZZ METHOD

Who says you can't teach Jazz? This book puts an end to that myth! There are certain basic chords and rhythms used in the make up of Jazz. And since these elements do exist, they can be simply taught.

ORGAN PARTY BOOK

Need a special tune for an occasion? This book contains selections for holidays, celebrations, parties, weddings and every type of happy occasion.

POPULAR CHORD DICTIONARY

This chord dictionary shows the notation, fingering and keyboard diagrams for all of the important chords used in modern popular music.

ROCK 'N' ROLL ORGAN BOOK

The rhythmic and bouncy quality of rock 'n' roll music has been authentically reproduced for organ. A rare treat for the adventuring organist.

YEAH! YEAH! YEAH!

The Liverpool Sound is here and it's the greatest! The Mersey Sound is the sensation of the year! Here are songs in this style and they are fabulous!

Alfred Publishing Co., Inc.
16320 Roscoe Blvd., Suite 100
P.O. Box 10003 • Van Nuys, CA 91410-0003
www.alfred.com

INTRODUCTION

FOR THE STUDENT: This material is part of the worldwide Suzuki Method of teaching. Companion recordings should be used with these publications. In addition, there are piano accompaniment books that go along with this material.

FOR THE TEACHER: In order to be an effective Suzuki teacher, a great deal of ongoing education is required. Your national Suzuki association provides this for its membership. Teachers are encouraged to become members of their national Suzuki associations and maintain a teacher training schedule, in order to remain current, via institutes, short-term programs and long-term programs. You are also encouraged to join the International Suzuki Association.

FOR THE PARENT: Credentials are essential for any teacher you choose. We recommend you ask your teacher for his or her credentials, especially those relating to training in the Suzuki Method. The Suzuki Method experience should be a positive one, where there exists a wonderful, fostering relationship between child, parent and teacher. So choosing the right teacher is of the utmost importance.

In order to obtain more information about the Suzuki Method, please contact your country's Suzuki Association; the International Suzuki Association at 3-10-15 Fukashi, Matsumoto City 390, Japan; The Suzuki Association of the Americas, P.O. Box 17310, Boulder, Colorado 80308; or Summy-Birchard Inc., c/o Warner Bros. Publications, 15800 N.W. 48th Avenue, Miami, Florida 33014, for current Associations' addresses.